# The Reason Why You Were Born

## 2014 Edition

**Written in the style of an easy to read
'Letter to a friend'**

**Outlining Spiritual Knowledge
Truth and Wisdom**

## James McQuitty

**Other recent titles by James McQuitty**

The Complete Guide to Spiritual Astro-Numerology
Help Yourself to a Better Life
Know Yourself
The Wisdom Oracle

Where I use the words *should* or *must* in this book it is purely for convenience and is not intended to be a dogmatic statement. I recognise and appreciate the fact that we all have freewill and, ultimately, are responsible to no one but ourselves.

**www.jamesmcquitty.com**

# Contents

# Foreword

Dear friend, there are certain fundamental facts of life that are so vitally important to recognise that you, and everyone else upon this planet, really should have been taught them from childhood.

The significance of these facts is such that as you read what I have to say within these pages, the knowledge contained may very well change your entire outlook on life.

It is knowledge that I have been privileged to discover during my lifetime; and I can honestly say that it has enhanced and given greater meaning and purpose to my life.

You may ask, 'From where does this knowledge come?' The answer is that initially, some of it came to me through my deep contemplations and intuitive ability to discern fact from fiction. Other aspects I learned from numerous spiritual scholars who long ago verified the validity of the teachings.

It is also knowledge that has been repeated on many occasions by those who have gone ahead of us to higher realms of consciousness and wisdom, to which we all gravitate after the demise of the physical form.

My friend, life *is* eternal, and such realms truly *do* exist; the proof of this has been given to me on countless occasions.

Throughout the centuries spirit guides from these higher realms have returned to speak to us through entranced mediums, to prove the continuation of life, to tell us of their realms and share wisdom. This communication continues today, and in the conversations that I and many others have had with them, they have confirmed my beliefs.

By sharing this understanding with you, I hope that it will enlighten your pathway, enabling you to make greater sense of your own life and this world, and shed some light on your future states beyond. I can say without doubt that your physical life does have meaning, and that it serves a purpose that you *will* one day appreciate.

One of my desires is for you to realise that you, on a higher level of consciousness before birth, were actively involved in planning many of the experiences that you have and will encounter in your physical lifetime.

I would also like you to realise that how you live your life carries responsibility; and to recognise the 'bigger picture,' that is, how and why things happen, and the part that you play in shaping your own destiny.

You may not realise just how far you have already journeyed in your spirit evolution, so within these pages I will also include my understanding of this. It is knowledge that *is* important, for it highlights the interconnectedness of *all* life.

It is my greatest hope that the knowledge which I will herein present to you, and kindred teachings, will one day become common knowledge, and that this will help to unite all people. For we *are* all the same: *eternal souls* with identical origins, undertaking the same journey, in our own unique way.

The time of awakening is now. For everyone to recognise that we *are* all connected; all part of the same energy that so often is called God, the Great Spirit, or one of many other names for the Power that *is* life itself.

Once you have read this, if you feel that you would like to confirm my discoveries, I would encourage you to investigate further with a discerning but open mind, as I have done, and I am confident that your own conclusions will closely mirror my findings.

Remember at all times that your true higher status is that of an eternal being; and this will help you to better cope with life's challenges.

# Chapter One
# The Spiritual Facts of Life

My friend, I will start by outlining for you what I consider the most important spiritual facts of life. I believe that people would live in greater harmony if these facts were taught from childhood. The order is of no real significance, for they all interrelate.

### 1. Life is Eternal

'Death' is simply the shedding of the physical form…

### 2. Incarnation
### The Reason Why You Were Born

Is to undertake spiritual lessons that are contained in life experiences; and it is through these that the vibration of the soul is quickened (increased or raised) so that it can progress to higher levels of expression…

### 3. Reincarnation

Many physical forms or lifetimes are experienced in the evolution of the soul…

### 4. Universal Laws

Are eternally in operation; with the *Law of Karma* bringing balance to the soul…

On the following pages I will shine some light on each of the above...

# 1. Life is Eternal

'Death' is simply the shedding of the physical form...

My friend, you, as *all* life forms do, will survive the passing of your physical form. The physical body will perish, or return to nature, but the energy being that motivates it (which is the real or true you), is an immortal aspect of the Power that, as I have said, is so often called God.

This eternal aspect that is the real you, may also be called a *soul* or *spirit.* A title that more often is bestowed after one has passed from the physical realm. Although you are in fact already an *eternal soul* temporarily linked through the physical body for reasons that I will come to later.

Your brain, as highly sophisticated as it is, is an organ that will perish upon the death of your physical body. Whereas your mind, which to degree links through the brain when we are incarnate, is the faculty and consciousness of your spirit, and can operate upon many levels of consciousnesses at the same time.

People are mostly aware of the conscious level, that which does indeed interact through the brain; while you most likely have some understanding of the subconscious level of the mind, which is responsible for many bodily functions without conscious thought, such as breathing, and the pumping of the heart. While the subconscious mind is also a storehouse of information that can sometimes be accessed under hypnosis or through meditation.

Your mind, at all layers or levels of consciousness, is indestructible, so it will continue to exist and operate, whilst retaining all meaningful memories, after the death of your physical body. Mind and spirit are inseparable, and are part of what is sometimes seen as the aura.

To understand life after death in more detail than faith and trust alone, (although personal proof can be forthcoming via a medium), it helps if you understand a little about vibrations.

Don't worry, my friend, I'm not going to speak in technical terms, because such things are beyond me! You will be familiar with TV, radio and mobile phone signals, which are transmitted on higher frequencies of vibration than the physical senses can directly perceive.

Their vibrations are transmitted through the atmosphere at the same moment, passing through the same space as each other, through buildings and our own bodies, yet they generally do not interfere with one and other. They only do so when they are transmitted on the same or a similar frequency of vibration, causing interference with each other.

The spirit is the same in that it functions on a much higher frequency of vibration than the physical form or senses. Therefore, in most circumstances, it is unseen or heard by us, just as we do not physically see or hear TV, radio or mobile phone signals, and can only do so when they pass through a suitably attuned receiving medium, a device that transforms the signals into something that we can physically see or hear.

As I have said, life is eternal, and when you pass from your physical form your soul will transcend to a higher realm or dimension of consciousness that is generally called the 'spirit world.'

Those souls residing in the spirit world can communicate with us. It is not easy, because they are living in higher dimensions and functioning at increased rates of vibration.

More commonly they do so by lowering their rate of vibration to a suitable frequency, so that they can attune to the same frequency as the human mediums upon earth who are attempting to raise their personal vibrations, and through telepathic thought communicate with them. It is rarely a precise attunement, mediums are not mechanical as our TV's, radios and phones are, so cannot be fixed to receive at a certain frequency; their receptivity is constantly in a state of flux, as they attempt to interpret and relay the telepathic communications. This link may pass images, thoughts or feelings, mind to mind. Some mediums, as I detailed in my book: *Over the Rainbow*, are naturally more adept at this than others.

I remember the first time that I witnessed a demonstration of mediumship. It was in 1967, when I was just 16 years of age. I attended because I had a natural sense of curiosity, and wanted to know the truth: whether or not we did survive 'death,' because to me it seemed an important thing to find out!

So off I went one evening to the old co-op hall in Peckham Rye (London), and nervously sat near the back! I was a somewhat shy youngster, so I was hoping that the medium would not speak to me. I did not go to receive a personal message; I just wanted to know the truth!

The medium was Jessie Nason, and she was one of the best of her generation. During her time she demonstrated at the Royal Albert Hall and on television. I doubt that she would have remembered her demonstration that evening in the co-op hall in front of perhaps 30 people, but I have never forgotten! The messages she delivered to a number of those present, all with clear evidential proof of survival, certainly convinced me of the fact that 'death' was not the end of life!

Since then, I have received personal messages and further proof of survival through many different mediums on hundreds of occasions. I have also had plenty of experiences myself! The first was in 1986 in Forest Hill, London. It was around 3am one morning when a translucent spirit lady walked into my bedroom, glanced around and then 'disappeared.' The same event repeated itself the very next night, but on this occasion it was a somewhat younger looking spirit lady.

From this time onwards, I have regularly seen spirit 'visitors,' and sometimes spirit animals, and heard the ringing of different bells and other raps and taps, during the night. The visitors are not trying to scare me, just to let me know that they are present.

Perhaps my most memorable experience of seeing a spirit person occurred around 10 years ago. Once again, I awoke to see someone, but on this occasion the glow of light that was visible made the person quite clear. He appeared Greek or Roman, with shoulder length wavy hair, and was dressed in flowing white or lightly coloured robes. In his hand he was holding a long staff. He seemed to smile towards me, looking quite pleasant or amiable, then, after what seemed an age (perhaps a full minute) he eventually faded from my vision.

A day or two later, I was due to meet a couple of friends, both mediums, who at the time lived in Portsmouth. Through them, I learned that the visitor was Asclepius, who in Greek mythology was deified as the god of medicine. He was considered the son of the god Apollo and Coronis.

Asclepius informed me that he was very much a man, but that he did use the curative properties of nature, the plants and herbs and such like, which he had acquired, in his healing ministry. Because he had great success, after he passed the stories about him became more exaggerated, until in legend he was considered a god.

He visited me to let me know that he, or his spirit group, was going to be working with me whenever I practiced the art of healing. It was a lovely message to receive. Before he departed on that occasion he placed a large snake around my shoulders. The 'rod of Asclepius' (similar to the caduceus), the snake wrapped around the staff, is associated with healing. At one time the two appear to have been separate symbols. The significance of the snake, or serpent, and the shedding of its skin, has been interpreted as symbolising renewal and rejuvenation.

# 2. Incarnation
## The Reason Why You Were Born

Is to undertake spiritual lessons that are contained in life experiences; and it is through these that the vibration of the soul is quickened (increased or raised) so that it can progress to higher levels of expression...

My friend, the aforementioned summarises why you are now upon the earthplane; if I wanted to be even more concise I could say, 'the reason for incarnation is for the evolution of the soul.'

Here, the word *soul* feels more appropriate than *spirit*. The *spirit* is the energy that empowers all life; the *soul* can be used to denote our individuality. We are all spirit, with our own unique individualism reflected in our soul essence.

The object of all earthly existence is that the spirit is to be quickened, its vibration raised. It is why you are here, so that through a variety of circumstances that life incarnate presents us with, your soul, which is the eternal you, will be enabled to express the latent qualities of the Power that lay at the core element of your being. All life is endowed with these qualities, but each of us needs to reveal them, recognise and learn to express them, for ourselves; this could also be described as finding and awakening your true self. But before we can do so, we need to learn and develop wisdom; and this is so that we not only recognise the power within, but learn to express it wisely. This, we must first do at the slowest level of vibration, which is physical matter.

Often, at the physical level of expression, the spiritual lessons we need to encounter so that our soul vibration can be quickened, come to us when we are confronted with difficulty and adversity. Although it would be hoped that most people will also experience happy times, and find friendships and love; to find pleasure in caring for and sharing with others; these moments also helping to teach and enlighten us as they light the pathway.

Although symbolically, it can be said, that it is not during times of sunshine that the soul is quickened. It is in the hazards and challenges, the difficulties, the hurdles and the obstacles. So often we face suffering, sorrow or difficulties; but these are the challenges that have to be met, accepted and overcome.

To continue with the metaphors, it can be said, that a storm can often do more to help you to spiritually grow and unfold than clement conditions. It is only in the darkness that you can find the light; and through the experiences you encounter your soul can advance.

I'll stop with the metaphors now, I expect you get the point!

It is for these reasons that the soul incarnates to experience a series of 'lessons,' as they are called, that will enable us to grow, unfold and develop, and to achieve the progress that will prepare us for the next stage upon the eternal journey. The lessons are not complicated; they are experiences that embrace aspects of charity, compassion, courage, dedication, faith, forgiveness, generosity, honesty, kindness, patience, responsibility, self-love, and ultimately unconditional love, and most likely more. Through them we progress to become finer (higher vibrational) spirit beings.

The lesson of *charity* is not necessarily about finance, it is the development of a charitable soul. Becoming lenient and not judging others; giving freely from the heart, while recognising that we are all in essence loving souls.

The lesson of *compassion* beckons us to recognise others' distress, to offer unconditional love, to avoid being cruel in any way.

The lesson of *courage* invites us to stay calm when chaos or adversity strikes, to allow our higher soul aspirations to guide us, and never to fight emotion with emotion.

The lesson of *dedication* asks us to show commitment to a cause, mission or person; to set targets and, whenever possible, to meet them.

The lesson of *faith* is not one of blind faith, but about trusting and recognising that there is a purpose in all things. Trust in the Power and in your own self, for you are connected to all life.

The lesson of *forgiveness* is one of letting go of judgement, resentment and negative feelings towards others. Again, offer unconditional love, and remember that we are all loving souls at the core of our being, even when this is buried deep beneath the layers of materialistic discord.

The lesson of *generosity* encourages us to be unselfish, openhearted and liberal in our thoughts and actions.

The lesson of *honesty* is a test of character, of our level of integrity; can we be truthful and honest at all times? Not only when dealing with others, but with ourselves also. Can we follow the promptings of the heart and conscience and avoid temptation?

The lesson of *kindness* would have us treat others with respect, care and compassion; to show kindness, and encourage and support them so that we might draw the best from them.

The lesson of *patience* says take your time, stay calm, centred, and steadfast and bear what life presents, without complaint; be composed and remember that life unfolds as it must.

The lesson of *responsibility* would have us distinguish right from wrong with conviction, to recognise that we are our own keepers, in charge of our own soul growth. That nothing is gained by turning away from the spiritual facts of life. We need to see the pathway of the soul through the illusion of matter and follow it with love.

The lesson of *self-love* wants us to respect and honour ourselves, mind, body and soul; to be aware of our own worth in the universe as equal aspects of the Power.

The lesson of *universal love* asks for absolute acceptance so that we might love all, and without judgement to see good in all things; with no expectations of receiving love or anything else in return.

You may gather that there are many, many ways in which each of the lessons can be encountered and experienced, and therefore why it is impossible to do so without incarnating on numerous occasions.

To reach the level of attainment when you no longer need to return to earth is a long and at times painful journey of experience. But you, as all of us, will choose to undertake it in order to ascend the levels and realms of the spirit dimensions; and to climb the ladder we all start at the lower rungs and master these before we can progress to the higher.

On a personal note, one of the lessons that I am here to learn is 'patience!' Like all lessons, this one repeats itself time and time again! Astrologically speaking, the broader lesson that I am here to learn is that of 'love.' In a lovely little book by Joan Hodgson (White Eagle Publishing) she tells me that I am pre-eminently here to develop the higher mind. She adds that, "The true function of the advanced Sagittarian is to be guide, philosopher, friend and law-giver to his companions." She adds: "When he has found truth for himself he will speak words of consolation, wisdom and inspiration, and the light of love will shine through his life to help and guide others in need of help." I don't think that I am always such a shining light, perhaps I am a 60 rather than a 100 watt light bulb! I guess that I can only do my best to live up to such high ideals!

Each incarnation is like a diamond that has been moulded to the soul that enables us to reflect greater spiritual light. The opportunities that the 'higher you' has accepted and dealt with enlarge its experience so that the soul can radiate at a higher vibration which is a reflection of its refinement.

My friend, by now you may seek clarification upon where God and religion come into the picture? The answer is that what we commonly call God, as I said earlier, is the Spirit, the Power, and we are aspects of this living, loving energy. Individually, we can make our progression more arduous and requiring of more incarnations, but the overall Power is forever in a state of Perfection. The Power does not 'punish' nor need personified interference, universal laws keep things in balance. Once aware of them, we can choose whether to live in harmony with them, or rile against them and draw to us the consequences. The choice is entirely our own to make.

As for religion, my friend, it so often serves no meaningful purpose, other than as a social outlet. On the one hand it does encourage love; but on the other some of its teachings remain a relic of ancient times, when people lived in fear of the elements. Today, many religions fear and even suppress spiritual truth, for it undermines them by challenging the need for such institutions. In many ways, belonging to a particular religion can be a geographical 'accident' of birth! We are assured by those who are already resident in higher states of life that you do not need to belong to a religion to gain admission to their realms; you will quite naturally progress there upon your physical passing. In fact, I ought to be saying that you will return there, for it is where you came from and have returned to many times previously. At what level you initially find yourself, will be a direct reflection of the lifetime that you have just experienced. There are higher and lower levels, relatively glorious and those darker and undesirable! But no one is damned or stuck for eternity on any level. So, fear not my friend, the pathway is eternal and glorious beyond the mortal dreams of humankind.

Between incarnations you may spend many years at a level of progression that befits your vibrational 'status.' Details of life in such realms as the 'Astral' have been given in a number of books, and I'm sure that many a happy reunion in 'heavenly' surroundings is enjoyed by the majority of people. But eventually, we are told that there always comes a time when each soul chooses to continue their climb up the spiritual ladder of progression. After all, without any challenge or purpose, even 'paradise' must lose its appeal.

I understand that when this time arrives, when the soul desires to make further progress, guidance comes. Then, with the help of one's soul group (those who are like spirit family), the plan for another round of experience is formulated with necessary lessons incorporated. The blueprint for the life plan can be very detailed, with many a secondary plan to allow for the freewill decisions of the earthly consciousness and the ever-shifting patterns that are interwoven by a great many different souls who may be intending to interact during the particular incarnation.

The interactions may be planned to help more than one party learn a particular lesson. Sometimes the pathways cross and forge a lifelong link and sometimes they are very brief encounters, like ships that pass each other in the night. We may all be able to reflect on a latter such occasion, when we have met someone very briefly and they have said or done something that affected or even fundamentally changed our lives? Whether at a physical level we view the circumstances as beneficial or tragic, the encounter may well have been planned prior to birth.

On a physical level of consciousness, we do not like every experience of life. Some we will consider enjoyable or satisfying, others will be less welcomed but may prove equally, if not more, beneficial to the advancement of the soul.

Spirit sages tell us that ultimately, there is no right or wrong! No good or bad; just experiences. It is how we cope, how we react, do we face each challenge as best we can, or do we cower away and say, "poor me?" Herein is one answer as to how we can progress more successfully through our incarnations; although I'm not suggesting that it is in any way easy!

If you would like to read more about pre-birth life planning and how incredibly courageous we can be, then *"Your Soul's Plan"* by Robert Schwartz is worth reading along with two books by Michael Newton *"Journey of Souls"* and *"Destiny of Souls."*

## 3. Reincarnation

Many physical forms or lifetimes are experienced in the evolution of the soul…

My friend, symbolically, you are presently just the portion that shows above the waters, below you are far greater and connected to the whole ocean of spirit life.

Souls generally seek to progress through the experiences undertaken during a succession of physical lifetimes (known as "reincarnation").

Upon passing, most people are initially guided to the astral realm. A realm said to be similar to the earthplane. Teachings say that it is like this because the collective thoughts and expectations of people are still focused upon the experiences and surroundings that they have just vacated, and that these shape the reality that they next experience.

After a period of adjustment, there comes a time when the soul needs to reflect upon the experiences of the most recent lifetime upon the earthplane. We are told that some people experience this as though watching a TV or cinema replay of their lifetime. During this time they see with 'soul understanding' the impact that their lifetime had, not only upon themselves, but also upon others. Realisation comes to them of how they may have progressed, where they have not, and whether they have either cleared or added karma.

Having awakened soul understanding of their lessons and karmic balance, there comes a time when the soul is ready to undertake another round of experience through incarnation; for they clearly understand in what way their soul needs to progress. This is discussed with their soul group, often with the help of more advanced guides, to determine the best course of action. In other words, what sort of incarnation would best facilitate experiences that would teach the lesson(s) that the soul next seeks to encounter in their spirit progression.

My friend, we are informed that the whole planet, in fact the entire universe, is involved in this same process, at different levels of progression. Furthermore, to greater or lesser degree, we serve each other, and at a soul level of consciousness, service is joyously interwoven in our life plans, whether or not we learn to recognise this at the physical level of consciousness.

We help each other as teachers and guides in numerous ways. Even those who seem rather unpleasant may be engaged in service. For how do we know whether or not they are in our lives to teach us a valuable lesson? Are the domineering tyrants attempting to teach us to stand-up for ourselves and not allow others to dominate us? Is the gentle soul there to teach us compassion, charity of soul, unconditional love and forgiveness? We need the contrast upon earth; for it is only through this that the soul is challenged to awaken its inner light of reason and discernment and through such challenges or lessons to gain a sense of 'balance.' This helps us to retain our equilibrium, so that we do not judge right or wrong, good or bad, and ultimately absorb the lessons contained within our earthly experiences.

All life is connected to the whole ocean of spirit life. We are all willing participants in these acts of service, whether as the willing worker, carer, teacher, or in some self-sacrificing capacity, or in any other of the countless ways in which service can be rendered. Whether we are male or female, live many or a few years, are healthy, wealthy or their opposites in a lifetime is very often determined before birth; in eternity, we experience both ends of every spectrum. The choices are made to suit the particular incarnation and to help balance the energies of the soul.

Red Cloud, a Native American Indian guide, when asked what the first law of spirit life is, said: 'The first law is universal love.' This is why, when in spirit, with awareness and understanding raised to a higher level of consciousness, we are happy and willing to be of service to each other; even to the point that a soul will incarnate to a lifetime of suffering, poverty, depravation, humiliation, torment and sorrow, in order to help teach one or many souls, the lesson(s) they need to experience.

Even diseases such as AIDS can, at a higher level of consciousness before birth, be chosen to help the soul through a particular life lesson and, at the same time, they very often help to teach many others. The sufferer may well be required to recognise that regardless of the disease, they are a worthy soul and deserving of love. So it may be that as this recognition comes to the sufferer, they spiritually progress. Lessons are also learned by observers and those more directly involved, as they also recognise this, and that no blame or shame should be attached to the sufferer.

My friend, over the years I have been fortunate enough to discover snippets about a number of my own past lives. The first one that I will mention will also highlight how initially frustrating some communications can be! But I believe this is because our spirit friends do not want to lay everything on a plate for us; sometimes we need to keep searching for aspects of truth along whichever pathway we are drawn.

Over a period of perhaps fifteen years, a number of mediums would ask me if I had any connections with Canada and the sea. (At times, it got to the point that it was the first thing that some would say to me!) I could never really answer, "Yes," in any meaningful sense; I do love living by the sea, and I did once have a girlfriend from Toronto, but that was about it – as far as I knew!

However, all eventually made sense when a few friends and I visited a medium in Ventnor, Isle of Wight. Her name was Margo Williams, whose guide specialised in telling people about their incarnation before the current one. During the sitting, the guide told me that in my previous incarnation I was born in Canada, and lived by the sea where sailing ships harboured. As a child in that lifetime, I was apparently fascinated by the ships and spent many hours at the seafront watching them coming and going. My father passed when I was 14 years old, and my mother remarried a man who at the time I did not like. So I stowed away on one of the trading ships! (What a crazy youngster I was in that lifetime!). As was inevitable, I was soon discovered, but rather than putting me ashore, the crew 'adopted' me as their cabin boy. Thus began a lifetime at sea that eventually saw me become captain of another trading ship. I reconciled my relationship with my mother and stepfather and had a wife and family. The lifetime (1850-1910) ended in a storm at sea when the ship went down. No blame was attached

to me; the weather conditions were apparently
unexpected.

## 4. Universal Laws

*Are eternally in operation; with the Law of Karma
bringing balance to the soul...*

My friend, many people embark upon a personal
spiritual journey of discovery and soon satisfy
themselves that there is indeed 'life after death,'
that we *all* survive the demise of the physical body.
Through one or more mediums they receive
evidential communications that convince them of
this fact. They also learn that their loved ones are
living in a loving environment and that when their
own time comes, they will be able to spend time
with them. Having reached this elementary level of
understanding, some people then cease their
pursuit of spiritual knowledge. However, by
presuming that they have all the understanding
they need, they so often miss what is far, far more
important.

This is because the fact that we all survive 'death'
is merely the foundation stone, the first step,
towards understanding knowledge that is far
greater. An important aspect of which is the 'Law of
Karma,' which is a universal, natural or spiritual law
that could also be called the 'law of equilibrium or
balance.' Karma is a Sanskrit-Indian word that
basically means the eternal balancing of the soul
which can be carried through many incarnations.
Upon earth, practically everyone born will carry
unresolved karma that they may be seeking to

rebalance in their current incarnation. This is known as a person's karma, or their karmic debt.

Natural law is like the perfect boomerang, what you send out, whether love or hate, kindness or evil, good or bad, eventually, it will always return to you.

Humankind's inhumanity towards each other seems eternal; wars are fought because of greed and ignorance. When people 'wake up' spiritually and recognise the truth, that we are all linked, all part of one eternal power, all responsible and accountable for our actions, they will recognise the futility of what has gone before, and begin the transformation of planet earth into a more loving environment.

Motive and accountability applies not only to how we treat other people, but equally to how we behave towards the animal kingdom and the environment. The needless suffering that humankind inflicts upon animals inevitably creates its own karmic debt, as does the destruction of the environment and natural resources of the planet for material gain. We are all one, what we give out always returns to us; it is the law of karma.

Understanding and respecting this universal law, by living your life as harmoniously as you possibly can with all other forms of life, ensures that you do not inadvertently hinder your personal spiritual progression. This is the reason why I share these facts with you, my friend. The law of karma is not your nemesis; it carries no malice, and is quite neutral in its outworking. It simply operates according to the nature of the spiritual universe. You therefore have no need to fear the law; but I feel that you, as all beings, deserve to have knowledge of it for your own sake.

Under the 'umbrella' of the law of karma is the 'Law of Cause and Effect,' which is more immediate in its outworking. For instance, you will recognise that if you put your hand in an open fire (cause) you will quickly burn yourself (effect).

Yet the law of karma holds greater significance; our spirit guides teach us that karmic law is linked directly with the unfolding consciousness of individuals. So it is not only our actions that affect us, but what we need to experience. We also carry personal responsibility for everything we think, say and do, and it is one thing to undertake an action in ignorance and quite another to do so in knowledge and understanding; our motives are important and carry an impact. The further we move up the spiritual ladder of unfoldment, the more responsibility we carry, and the greater the impact of karmic law.

You may have questioned why some people are born with a physical deformity or mental abnormality; others into poverty or disease or famine? Very often, this is the result of karmic law and the soul has chosen such an experience for the particular incarnation, because they are the conditions which it knows will facilitate the greatest lessons being learned to enable service to be rendered and the soul balance to be restored. For only when the balance has been restored and what has been accrued in a past life has been neutralised, can the soul move on to higher things and greater experience.

Karmic law may take but a few moments to outwork itself, or if one fails to advance in one lifetime, it may take many incarnations. When your awareness and wisdom enables you to think and to act in a responsible way, this quickens your soul vibrations and aids your progression towards the higher spirit world realms.

You are an aspect of the Power, (God, if you prefer), remember this, remind yourself of this fact on a daily basis if necessary, and you will find that your own thoughts and actions will more readily express your understanding. Then, you will choose your words and watch your actions with respect for all life, in the light of the responsibility which you have.

Provided that your motive is always true, selfless, and seeks that which feels spiritually right you will be unlikely to incur any karmic debt. It is only when you allow the lower emotions to dominate your thoughts and your actions that you may find yourself going astray. If you can stay attuned and alert to the promptings of the deeper and true conscience (not the ego of self-desire), this is the compass of the soul within, and it will always guide you to the truth. Follow it, listen to that inner voice, adhere to its promptings and you will find that it will always point you to the light.

My friend, never doubt the power of prayer, the sort that comes from the heart, not from ritual. It will always be heard and never ignored, although karmic law and the reasons for your birth, the lessons that you have agreed to experience, have to be borne in mind. Prayer can trigger the 'law of attraction' and may draw likeminded souls to you.

When used virtuously, it can also be considered the ultimate positive thought and can help one find inner peace and attunement to the higher aspirations of their own soul (this is often referred to as attunement to one's 'higher self').

The consequences of our actions, whether deliberately or inadvertently set in motion, can be immediate, but they may equally manifest much later during the same lifetime, when in the spirit realms, or in a future physical lifetime. Equally, the consequences may be spread over a mixture of physical, spirit, and future physical.

Your future will be that little bit brighter if you can eliminate as many negatives as possible, such as those of an inflated ego. Ultimately, of course, the choice in everything you think, say, or do, is always your own, because you have and always will have freewill, which is your right to choose. Generally speaking, if you are using your freewill wisely, you will be following a loving, caring and sharing pathway. Theoretically it is simple to do so, for if you follow your conscience and the inner sensing of your heart and intuition, they will guide you well.

My friend, through the process and law of reincarnation, until you have gone beyond the need for further physical incarnations, you will at some time in the future choose to reincarnate so that the soul, the real you, can once again seek to progress, and perhaps to help others in their progression, as they likewise may be assisting you. When this happens, you will bring with you the unresolved consequences of your past life actions. When the energies and interactions of an incarnation cannot be balanced in one lifetime the imbalance remains within the soul, and an attempt to rebalance the energies will be made in a future incarnation (not necessarily the immediate next). You will also gravitate towards a level appropriate to your vibrational status during your sojourns in the spirit realms.

The ongoing balancing is necessary firstly, as I have said, because the experiences, or lessons, that human incarnations teach cannot always be self-balancing in a single lifetime. It is necessary for us to experience a great array of lessons in a variety of circumstances and roles. If, for example, we experience a lifetime during which we are a strong-willed personality, because at a soul level we need to experience this, it is possible that in a subsequent incarnation, particularly if we have misused our willpower, we may also need to experience being on the receiving end of such a personality.

Secondly, and a reason why many souls carry unresolved or unbalanced karma (as I'm sure all of us have and perhaps do) is because we are not puppets of the soul whilst incarnate. We have freewill, the choice of whether or not to follow the inner guiding light of the soul, or to ignore it and pursue that which the physical ego craves. Unfortunately, as you will be aware, many people live solely by their materialistic desires, and this can be detrimental to their soul balance and result in further karma being accrued.

For this reason, for your **own** eternal sake my friend, I consider it very important to understand about your eternal nature and, as I have already mentioned, the natural universal spirit laws. For what we might view as negative actions may result in the need to experience far more physical lifetimes than would otherwise be necessary. As most of us are well aware, physical life can involve a great deal of suffering, whether physical, emotional or mental. This is not 'punishment' by any higher authority, but a natural aspect of physical experience. By understanding the universal laws, particularly karmic law, we can better appreciate why I say that it would be better if these facts were taught from childhood, for lack of understanding will not prevent their outworking. As you can appreciate, it is always better to live in the light of truth.

My friend, there are many other universal laws. They affect us in many different ways and aspects of our lives, and can interrelate with karmic law. For example, there are universal laws of action, attraction, compensation, correspondence, gender (which can change lifetime to lifetime), polarity, relativity, rhythm, vibration, the transmutation of energy, and the oneness of life. But the law of karma is the one that people need to understand more than any other at this time.

If you live in harmony with the natural laws this puts you in touch with the universal mind, opening many doors upon your pathway as life flows in tune with the infinite (The Power). The key is service and a loving heart. You will still face your challenges and darker moments, but with the light of truth in your aura you will be better equipped to rise above them.

# Chapter Two
# The Power

My friend, there *is* only one-energy behind all that exists, although it expresses itself in manifold ways throughout the universe. This is the source of life that, to repeat what I said earlier, people call God, The Great Spirit, and many other names. For simplicity I call this, "The Power." Spiritism describes this as 'The supreme intelligence and primary cause of everything.'

All expressions of universal energy, such as subatomic light particles that quantum scientists investigate, have the potential to develop mind. Every person at a soul level can also be considered a 'light being,' an aspect of The Power that has developed to the individualised level of consciousness.

At our outset, we emerged from the eternal energy reservoir of The Power. Symbolically, this is often referred to as *sparks from the fire of life*; while another metaphor puts it as *droplets from the ocean of life*.

Everything, every mineral, crystal, flower, plant, tree, insect, fish, bird, animal, and human, together with every star and planet (of which there are countless billions), the entire known and unknown universe, on all frequencies of vibration, are expressions of The Power.

You may gather that The Power also has an inseparable underlying mind. So in spiritual reality the universe is eternally part of one supreme, omnipresent mind that from our physical observation appears to subdivide so that each aspect or particle can find expression within the whole.

As I have said, we are such expressions, and as we evolve and move up the spiritual ladder, our consciousness and rate of vibration increases, as does the intensity of our light and this is expressed as colour in what is called the 'aura.' The collective aura comprises many levels of being, often called 'energy bodies' that go to make up our whole; these include the physical, etheric, astral, mental and spiritual.

Through the vast process of spiritual evolution we have progressed to individualised consciousness. Yet as eternal beings our progression can have no end. In the fullness of time we will progress to an expanded level of consciousness, to one that at our present stage of attainment would seem a level of super-consciousness. Even then, we will become aware of still vastly greater potentialities. The creative expression of The Power is part of us, and as our awareness grows, so shall we express our own understanding of that same creative energy.

The Supreme Mind is the directive aspect of creation, and our own minds are aspects of this. Through this constant mind-energy link, we too can gain access to infinite knowledge, and this is often referred to as looking at the Akashic records. Everything we say or do makes an impression upon the ether; it creates an eternal energy imprint, a permanent record. Because of this, everything that has ever happened, to each individual person and to the planet can be reviewed. Between incarnations it is the Akashic records that allow us to review our recent lifetime upon earth. However, those who are still upon earth who are able to access the records, like those in spirit, can only become aware according to their own level of attainment.

As we add one level of awareness to the next, another can be glimpsed and then gradually, through experiences, be slowly absorbed within our understanding. Then, as we extend our awareness, yet another level will open for us; thus gradually our level of consciousness will expand. Any desire for greater understanding begins spiritual growth and naturally brings its own progression.

The entire universe is experiencing this same development that can also be described as the 'unfolding of consciousness.' It is in a continuous state of vibration and is occupied throughout by innumerable life forms or life-streams at varying states of consciousness. There is no such thing as isolation; not from our fellow humans, or from animals and all within nature, to the farthest reaches of the universe; everyone and everything is linked and part of the same supreme mind and power.

## The Seven Rays

The Power is said to radiate seven major light rays, or vibrations of the one energy. From these are said to come another seven, and from these another seven, ad infinitum in a downward spiral.

Effectively this gradually lowers the interconnected vibrations from the dizzy heights of the supreme mind to the lowest expression of matter.

Every facet of creation likewise has seven expressions; all are microcosms of the macrocosm that is the whole. This is expressed throughout life, for instance, the seven colours of the spectrum are reflected through our own seven finer energy fields. It might be that the seven major light rays of the universe are reflected from stars and planets by subatomic light particles that serve as carriers through the cosmic ocean of life?

# The Ether

Another expression of The Power is known as 'The Ether,' which effectively is a matrix of energy that links all creation. When we recognise this interconnectedness it becomes easier to understand how astrology, the alignment of the planets and much more that takes place in the galaxy and unseen universe, can and does affect upon us to some degree. For the ether, the spirit elements that occupy all space are the cosmic ocean that links the universe as one unfolding consciousness; therefore we, to a degree, affect the farthest point imaginable, and what happens everywhere else, likewise affects us.

The ether has also been described as *The Field*, and the *Universal Web* or *Energy Grid*. In whichever way described, all refer to a network of energy with underlying mind that is the fabric of existence.

*"The Field"* is also the title of a book by Lynne McTaggart, which details a number of supportive scientific investigations.

# Life Force Energy

Another way that The Power expresses itself is called the 'Life Force Energy;' and this is said to be the directing principle of life.

Matter, as we perceive it, is concentrated energy, the coming together of atoms at a slower rate of vibration. Within each atom are tiny subatomic particles, protons and neutrons, surrounded by electrons, so that the atom takes on the appearance of a mini solar system. When the elements of matter combine to form a body capable of sustaining life, such as our own, there is a natural magnetic attraction to an appropriate level of the life force energy that, throughout a healthy lifespan, will flow continuously and harmoniously to us at appropriate rates of vibration for each of our seven energy bodies. You may prefer to think of this as the link between spirit and matter, but in fact everything is spirit.

Life force energy has been recognised by some cultures for centuries; in India it is called, 'Prana,' and in China it is called, 'Chi.' It is present in the four elements of earth, air, fire and water. From the earth we take our food; the air we breathe; the fire is light or heat from the sun; and we drink water. The Chinese teaching lists five elements: wood, fire, earth, metal and water. While the art of energy healing, or 'energy cultivation,' otherwise known as: 'Chi Kung' (or Qigong) and similar practices, promotes or encourages the flow of energy into the body.

## Healing Energy

The Power can also be directed to us in the form of "Healing Energy." When we are unwell, depleted or lacking balance or harmony in our personal energy fields, if a request is made, then healing energy will come to us. The energy can come through the laying-on of hands, or through distant healing in response to prayer.

Healing energy is the power of life itself at appropriate rates of vibration to fit the circumstances or needs. Individuals refer to the energy under many different names, such as: universal, cosmic, natural, life-force, divine or spiritual healing energy.

The power exists everywhere within the universe, it is omnipresent, responding to thought (or prayer) or magnetic attraction that might be described as subconscious or unconscious thought. Effectively, energy 'healing' attempts to retune the energies, firstly in the aura; and this can lead towards a more harmonised balance within the composite being; encouraging emotional, mental and bodily healing. All, of course, is subject to prevailing karma and natural law.

I have had many personal experiences of healing. These include witnessing spirit surgeons perform surgery through entranced mediums, such as Stephen Turoff and Ray Brown, with excellent results.

A friend of mine had a protruding disc at the lower part of her back; it was very clear to see, and she regularly suffered pain as a result. I was in the same room and witnessed Stephen Turoff, entranced by Dr Khan I believe, appear to 'chisel' at the disc, then within a minute or two, lay his hands to cover the area. Very shortly afterwards, when he had finished and I examined her, the protruding disc had gone! All that was visible was a tiny mark that vanished by the following day. The pain, to a large degree, had also been alleviated.

An interesting demonstration of healing, or 'spiritual surgery,' which I witnessed in Seaton, Devon, was performed by Ray Brown, in trance. The spirit surgeon, Paul, who works through him, explained as he went along what was happening on the spirit side of life. Paul was not the only spirit or soul in attendance; he had his own team working with him.

The same can be said for Ed Pearson and Jenny Miller who used to work together as a team, but now work independently. When working together they said that for each 'operation' up to 14 spirit attendants were present, including specialist surgeons, technicians, nurses, anaesthetists etc. Their spirit surgeons, Matthew (with Ed) and Joshua (with Jenny) trained in the spirit world for 300 of our years to develop and perfect their skills in this work.

In July 2010 Ed and Jenny visited my home in Ryde, Isle of Wight, to demonstrate and practice, with positive, tangible results being reported by many of those who received help. During their demonstration I was sitting in the front row and could feel the warmth from a vortex of energy that surrounded them. They explained that their spirit team use this as their 'operating theatre.'

I think it would be fair to say that spiritual surgery is not miraculous or magic, or mystical in any way, although it may seem that way to those who reap the benefits! It is surgery that is simply beyond our present earthly understanding. It also embraces healing energies of The Power, with an understanding of the chakra energy points and meridian energy pathways that flow throughout our composite whole.

Perhaps the most famous healer of the twentieth century was Harry Edwards. He helped and healed thousands of people, many whose cases had been given up by orthodox doctors. The Harry Edwards Spiritual Healing Sanctuary which he founded at Burrows Lea, Shere, Guildford, Surrey, is still helping people today.

If you get the chance, my friend, do read *Harry Edwards* - The life story of the great healer, by Ramus Branch, it is an excellent biography of his life.


## Prayer

The power of prayer is real. Literally, it connects with The Power and draws forth an appropriate response. You can say a prayer for enlightenment as you read these words and The Power, and your own guides, may become noticeable to you? Perhaps you will experience this as a feeling of energy around your head, or in some similar way?

You can pray for all things, protection, guidance, strength, courage, whatever you need; you will never be ignored, although what comes will be that which is right for you at that particular moment in time.

Your soul growth is naturally of prime concern to The Power, so answers to all prayers, although never ignored, may not be forthcoming if that would interfere with your own, or that of another's, soul plan. The chosen experiences of the soul plan cannot be overridden by the power of prayer. In truth, no soul would want this to be so, because it would simply delay their soul growth and progression.

One of the universal laws is, "Like attracts like." It operates on the earthplane and in the spirit world realms. Therefore, your thoughts and prayers will draw to you like-minded souls from the spirit world. Feeling the attraction some will come out of curiosity, as friendly 'visitors,' to see what you are doing, while others will want to help you in some way.

Each of us has such souls around us, guides, angelic beings, helpers, relatives, friends new and old, even those connected to previous physical lifetimes; some come and go, others are with us throughout our time on earth. Pray to any or all of them, everyday, but more especially to The Power, and ask that healing energies go to everyone you know who is in need, not forgetting yourself, for you too are special and an equally deserving soul.

Like so many other people, I never used to take prayer seriously. To me it was something that 'religious' people did, and seemed rather meaningless! However, as I mentioned in my book: *Golden Enlightenment II*, whilst working in Saudi Arabia in 1980, I discovered for myself that it does connect with a greater power.

Having seen Egyptian work colleagues praying on their prayer mats, and looking as though they were gaining some peace and satisfaction from doing so, I decided to try prayer for myself. I was missing the comforts of home and feeling rather low, so thought "why not." Besides, it was in private when I tried, so nobody was going to laugh at me!

As soon as I started to pray to The Power, using the title God at the time (it really doesn't matter what name one uses), I felt surrounded by energy. I was amazed; it was such a tangible connection.

I think now that it was the energy of my guide White Cloud which I could particularly feel, and I am sure that he was delighted because, in a sense, it was the day that my spiritual illumination really began.

# Chapter Three
# The Spirit World Realms

My friend, there are a number of different spirit world realms. They have been given names, although these quite often differ from teaching to teaching. Within each realm are countless levels, like stepping stones or sub-divisions through the particular realm. As the soul evolves, the vibrations quicken to a higher rate, and we progress upwards through the levels and realms, one step at a time.

Some teachers call what is considered the highest realm the 'celestial;' below which are 'spiritual' and 'mind' realms. Further down is the realm that many people first gravitate towards upon their passing, one that I have mentioned earlier, and this is often called the 'astral.' While still further down the vibratory scale, there is the lower astral down to the dark and thoroughly undesirable levels of existence, the 'shadow-lands,' as they are sometimes called.

The earthplane itself is not disconnected from the spirit world, and can be considered the material end of the spirit world realms, for matter as you know is simply energy at a lower rate of vibration.

Since we do not generally see those who have passed, it is common to think of 'here' and 'there,' but the difference is simply one of vibration. Those in the spirit world realms still have form that is tangible to others at a similar level of vibration. Initially this is a reflection of their earthly appearance, only more vibrant, healthy, and without any deformities or damage that their physical form may have sustained during their earthly lifetime.

Some souls, perhaps because their understanding is limited, and sometimes because they fear what is to follow, do not want to 'move towards the light' that is so often seen upon passing. The light appears as a beacon towards their loved ones, and to the astral or whichever realm befits their vibrational status. Instead, they may remain within the orbit of the earthplane, and such souls are usually referred to as 'earthbound spirits.'

Sometimes this is because they have been frightened by a dogmatic religion into thinking that they are 'doomed to hell' or that they are in some way unworthy. Such belief systems can be difficult to overcome, while others may not accept that they have physically passed, and may believe that they are dreaming. Former family, friends, and guides often do try to help such souls, although we are told that some of them take much persuasion and reassurance before they finally accept that they have passed or that what they were told upon earth was incorrect. Then, such souls can be helped to progress.

There are other souls who are not truly earthbound, but choose (usually for a limited time after passing), to remain close to the earth. Often it is someone who wants to reassure a loved one that they are still living, albeit in spirit form. So they may attempt to be seen or heard in their former home or that of a relative, for instance. Sometimes they manage to cause some noise, a rap or tap, and whilst this may simply scare those remaining in physical form, this isn't their intention; it is often the only way that they can make their presence known. It may be the first tangible proof that the loved one has received that 'life after death' is fact not fiction. So although this 'first contact' may initially scare, it may lead to further investigation, which in turn can lead to a more enlightened understanding of the spiritual nature of all life.

A recently passed soul may be more readily seen or affect the material world, because the soul body is comprised of several layers of energy (as I referred to earlier), called 'energy bodies' or 'energy fields.' These layers interconnect, like the layers of an onion. At the highest or more spiritual end of the scale they are of a much higher frequency, while they gradually reach a lower frequency as they meet the physical form. The final layer that interlocks with the physical form is often called the 'vital' body. This is said to effectively 'intertwine' with the electromagnetic field that surrounds every living being upon this earthplane, and can more readily be called the 'aura.' Although the aura can also reveal higher spirit bodies, often it is only the lower vibrational aspects that are seen or detected by scanning devices. This 'vital' body is said to slowly 'dissolve' after passing, more speedily when the soul transcends directly to the astral. However, when a soul remains close to the earthplane, the dissolution is more gradual, and this vibrational embodiment enables the soul that has chosen to remain close to the earthplane more potential to be seen or influence material matter, because the vital body is so close in vibration to physical matter. It will particularly be seen by those more sensitive to higher vibrations or by anyone when their own sensitivity is attuned through a relaxed state of mind; for instance, when they are daydreaming or drowsy and half asleep.

'Seeing the light' is a more common experience than many people realise. Whilst still in physical form, many people remember 'out of body' visits to the astral realm via what is often called 'astral travelling.' Generally this occurs more to people as they physically sleep and some are able to retain fragmented or more vivid recollections of what they have seen and who they have met. There are also some people who can consciously initiate such excursions through an act of will and actively direct or influence their travels, enabling them to meet friends and guides on occasions.

Most, if not all, people journey to astral or higher realms whilst their physical body sleeps; while there, we no doubt enjoy meetings, and may discuss whether we are progressing as planned, and perhaps much more. A feeling of recognition and familiarity when we visit somewhere for the first time can very easily relate to having astral travelled during sleep in preparation for what is to physically follow. While there are also occasions when past life memories can be triggered by returning to somewhere that made a particular impression upon the soul. Equally, such experiences can be applied to meeting people for the first time. Some can seem very familiar to us, and more often indicate a past life connection. Our physical consciousness cannot generally remember past lives because the personality that we are now is unique to this lifetime. However, the individuality that is our soul retains those memories. Therefore, people who do remember or glimpse a past life memory do so by accessing a higher level of their being.

'Seeing the light at the end of the tunnel' and glimpsing the 'other side,' which is usually part of the astral realm, is a common recollection amongst those who have returned from what is called a 'near-death experience.' Many people report seeing relatives and friends who have previously passed, and how the colours are brighter and more vibrant than their physical counterparts, while they also report an overwhelming feeling of love. Often the experience closes when, from the spirit side, they are told that it isn't their time to pass, and the next thing remembered is waking in their physical body. Such experiences are not mass hallucinations, nor are they brought on by electrical impulses within the brain, as a number of TV psychologists would have us believe; (although, because the soul interconnects with the physical, it may cause this reaction). They are genuine 'close encounters' with those in the astral realm. To believe otherwise is to bury one's head in the sand with regard to overwhelming and undeniable proof which has always existed.

Eventually, it would be hoped, that all souls transcend to the spirit world realms. Once there, it would be impossible to guess how long it may take us to progress through to its highest realm. While we are assured that any desire to progress *will* draw to us those who are willing to teach and give advice. However, nobody can progress by desire alone, it has to be merited; and when it is, the frequency of soul vibration increases accordingly.

In the astral realm, we are told that the desires of the heart can be pursued; like meeting with relatives and friends from the recent incarnation, and indulging in whatever 'leisure' pursuits we wish and have earned the right to follow.

Even the basic pleasures of the earthplane can be indulged in, such as eating and drinking. But after a while, because the soul does not require material sustenance, such desires fade away. Some of my books, such as: *Golden Enlightenment II* and *Over the Rainbow* detail many more answers concerning spirit world life. Other authors have also supplied answers, and books like "*Life in the World Unseen*" and "*Here and Hereafter*" by Anthony Borgia, "*The Spirit's Book*" by Allan Kardec, and "*Wisdom of Ramadahn*" by Ursula Roberts, will add to your understanding.

The underlying foundation stone of progression through the realms is "service." This fact is stressed by spirit teachers who communicate with us from the spirit world realms. Quite often, I believe, this need not involve doing anything that one fails to find enjoyment or satisfaction in.

Although there are forms of service that, in the usual sense of the word, may not seem pleasurable, such as spirit rescue. An example of this would be when a volunteer undertakes a mission of mercy into the darker realms of the spirit dimensions. Such realms really do exist; souls drawn there being those who, in their karmic balance, have gone badly astray. Perhaps, when upon the earthplane, they were materialistic to the point that they caused suffering, or in any number of ways were cruel or severely harmed others' life plans.

Yet, I believe that there can be great satisfaction in this service, when those whom the volunteers seek to help, by way of education and encouragement, begin to show remorse and seek to atone for their actions and to move forward. I must stress that there is no judgement in the realms, it is the outworking of natural laws that determine one's place and the fact that such undesirable levels exist.

It is taught that there are, of course, countless ways in which one can serve, and it is through service that one progresses. Whenever we assist others, upon the earthplane or in the spirit realms in a selfless way, we increase our own sensitivity and, ultimately, as our own rate of vibration increases, we ourselves move forward to a higher expression of the spirit world realms. So service is a two-way process. By helping others we also help ourselves.

On recognising this, it may sound as though it devalues the process, for one might then question whether our service was truly offered as a loving gesture or was done more to benefit our own progression. Yet the spirit within understands "motive" and we can no more fool ourselves than we can others in the spirit world. Motive is the key. If the motive is pure then the effect will naturally follow. Tainted motives will obviously do little to increase one's rate of vibration.

The realm beyond the astral is often called the 'Mind realm.' At the mind level of spirit life and above are those who have progressed beyond the *need* to undertake any further incarnations upon the earthplane. We are assured that those who gravitate to the mind realm and above do not become 'pious' or 'holy' in attitude or action, as some religions may suggest. By evidence, that many of us have witnessed, a sense of humour is most certainly retained. If anything, I would guess that a greater sense of humour may prevail, as they have progressed to the point when they can more readily see the 'bigger picture' and realise how absurd our earthly thoughts and actions can be, while they remember that they too once thought and acted as so many upon earth do. One day, we too may look back and laugh at how we are today?

At mind level, by personal choice, service to those in the astral or upon the earthplane can occupy some of their time. We are told that there are groups dedicated to improving links with those upon earth in a continued attempt to provide evidence of survival, to give comfort through healing and to share spiritual philosophy. They seek to communicate and help us in the hope of awakening humanity to the greater truths of life. By so doing they try to assist our spiritual progression, so that we are not adversely swayed from our chosen pathways by the materialistic nature of the earthplane.

They do so because in so many cases, whilst they have forgotten their own life plan, people are not fulfilling the desires of their soul. Rather than living caring, sharing and loving lives, so often they are living for themselves, busy in material and physical satisfaction, without any true concept of what is to follow. Effectively, they are at odds with their own soul, and are living lives that have little understanding of the spiritual realities and no concept of universal laws.

Spiritual knowledge is not a secret intended for the select few; people deserve to know the truth of eternal life and of universal laws and of the future they sow for themselves. The Power does not ask you to guess the right pathway. The directional guidance is within spiritual mind and can manifest through conscience and intuition.

Sometimes people upon the earthplane choose to call those who are further progressed in the spirit world realms "spiritual masters." Yet, we are assured that no hierarchical system of domination exists in any of the spirit realms above the earthplane. They are merely the custodians of greater wisdom and understanding that, when we reach the right level, will be open to us; and by using it wisely they seek to guide, give advice and help in numerous ways.

Those who are further progressed are aware of our needs, and of the experiences we need to encounter to further our spiritual progression. They have trodden the same pathway themselves, perhaps long ago. Sometimes they see us making the same mistakes over and over again, often incarnation after incarnation, so like a loving parent they try to guide and give advice; although our freewill allows us the choice of whether we listen or ignore any guidance that comes our way.

Guidance from the realms often reaches us via our subconscious mind, from where it will, hopefully, filter into our conscious thoughts. Regrettably it seems that too many people ignore thoughts and ideas that suddenly formulate in their minds, or which reach them via their intuitive faculties (a gut reaction), and dismiss them as their imagination (or a nervous reaction). They appear so natural to us, happening as they do throughout our lifetimes, that it seems no one else is involved. They become 'guiding-thoughts' only if we allow them to be so.

My friend, perhaps in the majority of cases, the indoctrinated religious, scientific, social and family programming, with inflated materialistic values, is all too powerful for many to allow these guiding thoughts entry for proper evaluation. The programming causes people to dismiss as imagination anything outside of the perceived parameters of 'normal' or 'conventional' communication.

From childhood, the majority of people are brought into line with what is considered acceptable. Sometimes this is reasonable, for instance to prevent physical harm, but all too soon it becomes imprinted upon our thinking processes in a way that so often poisons us to spiritual reality. It denies us the true facts of life eternal, for our earthly teachers are ignorant of them. Society is then led blindly to travel down the material cul-de-sacs of spiritual frustration, caught up on the seemingly never-ending wheel of rebirth. It seems that only the lucky few are able to free themselves totally from the boundaries imposed by earthly indoctrination and misinformation. Even many loving souls with goodness in their hearts remain enslaved to systems or ways of life that restrict the way that they express themselves.

As I have previously mentioned, my friend, one such institution, under many different names with countless doctrines and dogmas, is religion. I hope and pray that you do not fall under its spell; for it has caused so much conflict throughout history. Religion could have served a useful purpose, if it had allowed the natural teachers, those who are mediumistic, or those who are attuned to their intuition to guide. Instead, we have permitted the materialistic and indoctrinated to preach what they wanted people to believe as certainty and fact so that the select few could keep themselves in positions of earthly power and control. After their transitions, such souls may well have many regrets and find themselves with plenty of karma to balance. The same can of course be said for many politicians and others in positions of power who work purely for their own material gratification, or to satisfy the demands of their inflated egos.

As I have intimated though, a time will come when they, and *you,* will have experienced every necessary 'lesson' and have balanced all karma on this plane. At this time, when you arrive back in the spirit world realms, you will never *have* to return to earth through incarnation. You could of course *volunteer* to be reborn to help others, if you so desired, but the personal necessity will have ceased. So only the courageous or most self-sacrificing of souls return, for once here, they could again become embroiled in karma.

# Chapter Four
# Angelic and ET Life

My friend, we are not 'alone' in this physical universe; life abounds everywhere! We are informed that there are millions (perhaps billions) of other planets where spirit beings take physical embodiment, if that is their pathway, and like us they can seek to progress through experiences. In addition, there are beings that, at this time in the evolution of their soul, do not generally incarnate into physical form.

## Angelic Life

I speak principally of those from the 'angelic line of creation,' as it has become known. 'Angel' actually comes from the Greek word 'angelos,' the basic meaning of which is 'messenger.' Angels, or angelic beings, have assisted all life upon earth from the very beginnings of the planet; although it is often in times of danger that their presence has been particularly noticed. It is said that every human soul, whilst incarnate in physical form, has a 'Guardian angel.' This angel is also known as the 'Recording angel;' and oversees the outworking of karma. Angels are concerned with the building of form in all kingdoms of life, from the mineral to the human. While those who guide us from the spirit world realms are concerned with the growth of spiritual consciousness. The two aspects are naturally interconnected and jointly considered when we plan any incarnation.

Whether spirit beings are from this planet, another, or from a different line of evolution, (which we are informed angelic life is), they are nonetheless equal aspects of The Power. All beings and all lines of evolution are on the pathway of progression that slowly takes us and them up the ladder of spiritual progression or unfoldment, to reach higher states of awareness and levels of expression.

In the angelic line there is an order of progression, just as there is in our own line through physical form. At the lower end of angelic expression are 'Nature spirits,' associated with the four elements of earth, air, fire and water. These include Fairies and Gnomes, who are concerned with the earth, and assist the flow of life force energies to plants and trees. Air spirits are often called 'Sylphs,' fire spirits: 'Salamanders,' and water spirits: 'Sprites' or 'Undines.'

At the Nature spirit level of expression they share a group consciousness, just as animals and those below this level do in the physical line. Above them are the angels who, like us, have attained individualised consciousness. While at the highest level of expression are the 'Archangels,' who we could perhaps equate with those from the higher realms of the spirit world. What I have outlined is an extremely basic 'structure,' and it is likely that there are many intermediary or sub-levels in the angelic line of life, just as there are many realms and levels upon our own pathway of progression.

Additionally, there are non-evolving etheric 'thought forms' that are generally called 'Elementals.' The angels create these through an act of will, by the power of their thoughts; Elementals, like nature spirits, are associated with each of the four elements of earth, air, fire and water. Those from the angelic line are sometimes called 'Devas,' the word coming from Sanskrit, meaning 'Shining ones,' because when seen, they so often appear as beings of bright light.

In the group stage of mind expansion it is believed by some teachers that a change in evolutionary life lines can occur. This can take a developing soul from the physical line of evolution, where they may, for instance, have reached the level of a bird, into the nature spirit line of evolution. This line will eventually lead the developing soul into individualisation as an angel. It is also reported that those from the angelic line can come into human form; although this is said to happen on rare occasions only. While those who have developed beyond any earthly karma progressing as a human soul, might also switch into the angelic line as an angel.

Essentially, of course, we are all *spiritual beings* regardless of the outward form through which we may manifest, and are all equal aspects of The Power.

Personally, as I mentioned in *Golden Enlightenment II*, some years ago I once saw an elemental figure coming from a quartz crystal. When it appeared to realise that it was being observed (and filmed), the little figure quickly submerged itself back within the crystal.

I also mentioned that a friend, whilst in an altered state of consciousness, would often see nature spirits, and that we could also converse with them. Most of those she linked with were fairies that looked like beautiful little girls about four inches tall. There was also the occasional Gnome, and a Pixie, who we were told works on the earth and potatoes.

Because there was a need at the time, when the lady was in an altered or trance-like state, I would channel healing energies to her. She was always able to recognise the presence of two angels, and she saw them as beings of light. Somehow, she knew that one was an angel of healing and that the other was her guardian angel.

My friend, if you would like to know more about angels and nature spirits then I would suggest that you read a couple of trance channelled "White Eagle" books, *Spiritual Unfoldment II* and *Walking with the Angels* (both are extremely informative).

## Angelic Hierarchies

We dwell in what, for obvious reasons, is called *The Physical Universe*. Some spirit teachings suggest that this universe was developed by a 'Logos.' A name or title given to an aspect of The Power that, at present, is so far beyond our comprehension, to be considered god like! The Logos is said by these teachings to be the directing intelligence behind all manifestation in this universe. While its own existence is considered a manifestation of The Power that dates back to pre-cosmic 'time;' in other words, before this universe existed. The Logos is also referred to as *God of this universe*, while in some teachings it is called the *Godhead*. The word 'Logos' comes from Greek, and basically means 'The manifested Deity who causes universes into being and life.'

The Logos is 'assisted' by an 'Angelic hierarchy' that 'in the beginning' were the 'Seven Rays of Creation.' These seven rays have been referred to by many different names, for instance: 'The Seven Angels round the Throne,' 'Archangels of Spiritual Light,' 'The Seven Silent Watchers,' 'Lords of Karma,' 'Lords of the Flame,' and 'The Elohim.' Names, of course, really don't matter, for they are far beyond earthly personality or ego.

The 'Seven Rays,' the rays that stream (or vibrate) from the highest expression of angelic life, are said to permeate the universe that abounds with vast legends of angelic life which assist the flow of energies and the development of form and consciousness. The scale of the hierarchy which descends from the Mighty Seven seems immense; with 'Solar and Planetary Archangels.' There are said to be four 'Higher Archangels' who are concerned with the four elements who also record or direct world, national, group and individual karma; overseeing the angels and nature spirits below themselves on the scale of angelic evolution.

Angelic life and form is etheric, non-physical as we would recognise it, and can live and express throughout the universe. Physical conditions present no obstacle or hindrance to them. It is therefore no surprise to learn that they are present on *all* planets. Each planet may vibrate at a sub-frequency of one of the Seven Rays and, assisted by angelic life, act like a receiving and forwarding station for the power that flows from the Mighty

Seven to encourage consciousness growth throughout the universe? Thus affecting not only human and angelic life, but every level from the mineral, so that form as well as mind advances and evolves in spiritual evolution. This adds further weight to the teachings of Astrologers, in that the planets affect us on all levels of being, physical, emotional, mental and spiritual.

Every planet has its own overseeing Archangel, including the Sun, which is said to be the 'domain' of the Archangel Michael. We are told that 'he' is a 'Sun spirit' and is the highest and leading Archangel in this solar system. Michael is often depicted as carrying the 'sword of spiritual truth.'

My friend, there is so much to learn about the higher life and creation. If you are so inclined, information concerning the spiritual hierarchies and a great deal more is detailed in the writings of Rudolf Steiner. You may be able to find a copy of a book by Roy Wilkinson titled: *Rudolf Steiner – An Introduction to his Spiritual World-view, Anthroposophy*.


## Extra-Terrestrial Life

There are countless planets in the universe which number in the billions. We will never have a way of calculating a true figure any more than we can measure the infinite universe.

In linear terms, one scientific source suggests that the universe is 13.7 billion years old! A mind-boggling figure which, if we had been incarnating throughout, would have allowed us to have experienced hundreds of millions of lifetimes each!

Spirit guides inform us that the universe is orderly, with universal laws and purpose to all that exists; there is nothing haphazard, random or out of place. Everything has reason; nothing 'appears' by its own volition; no planet solely creates itself; there is cause behind everything that happens and a directing intelligence.

Therefore one can conclude that every planet which we observe has reason behind its physical existence. Life as we recognise it will not develop on every planet, but who is to say that life which we are unable or perhaps incapable of recognising, is not present? There may be life forms, other than on earth, which are developing mind from the microcellular level of consciousness. Perhaps they are progressing through finer elements which our scientists would not recognise and could even be unique to a planet?

It should therefore be no surprise that extra-terrestrial life forms with more advanced technologies than ourselves not only exist, but are capable of observing and if they so wish, interrelating with us.

Fear of such beings is rather irrational, as it would be hoped that, in the majority of cases, technological advances would progress more or less at the same pace as spiritual understanding. Although we are told, that some are friendlier than others.

If I remember correctly, I once heard White Feather (a Native American spirit guide), speak on the subject. He suggested that an openly acknowledged extra-terrestrial 'arrival' may take place later this century. I think the 2060's where mentioned; although this may be subject to whether or not the combined vibrational energies of those upon earth, at that time, have risen sufficiently (as anticipated). When the energies are more loving, it may encourage their arrival.

By this date I, for one, will have long since passed to the spirit world realms. If you can do so, please pass this information on to the younger generation and encourage them to welcome, without any fear, extra-terrestrial visitors when they do arrive, as such a time will usher in an exciting new chapter in the history of planet earth.

Incidentally, a number of excellent White Feather books, such as: *The Enlightened Soul*, containing spiritual philosophy and answers to a great many questions, have been produced by his medium Robert, and Amanda Goodwin.

# Chapter Five
# The Evolution of the Soul

The evolution of the soul is an eternal journey that has many beginnings but no true end, only intervals before the next 'adventure' begins.

## Group Soul Progression

Your spirit energy has already progressed or developed through various stages of mind growth; from the lowest to the human level of *individualised soul*.

This may seem an incredible concept, but let me assure you that you *are* an incredible being. You, or the spirit energy that eventually became you, has progressed from the bottom rung of the ladder (upon earth this is the mineral level of mind), through the chain of evolution to the human level of consciousness.

It may interest you to know that throughout our physical lifetimes we also assist the chain of evolution. This is because our own bodies act as host vessels for lower forms of consciousness existing at a microcellular and mineral level of mind. Over the course of unlimited time these lower minds, aspects of their own particular group souls, will also progress through higher forms that will eventually lead them to individualisation. Everything in creation is a microcosm of a macrocosm, a mirror image of the universe. We are *all* aspects of The Power, consciousness within Supreme Consciousness.

A flower grows and then it withers and 'dies,' or so it seems? The truth is that the form 'perishes' to a point when it is no longer sustainable and the spirit essence that motivated it then moves on. Therefore, on your climb up the ladder of mind, this is another form that your own spirit essence, in the group soul stage, may very well have passed through.

My friend, some people find this concept very difficult to accept, yet in a sense it is little different from a seed developing to become a plant, or a human embryo becoming a person. If you did not have to progress from the lowest level of mind, how could your mind have reached its present level of consciousness? By luck some would say, a cosmic fluke, while those indoctrinated by many religions would say, by God's will.

The fact is that no element of 'fluke' exists in creation, life is not 'pot luck;' it is earned, from the bottom rung of the ladder to the very top, if such a peak exists. Initially, as part of a group, we have progressed through form at all levels of vibration, from the mineral through vegetation, insect, bird and animal to human. I have not listed all forms, for you can fill in the gaps for yourself, where for instance you think a dolphin or a reptile might 'rank' in order of mind, as it is difficult to be absolutely sure. There are also levels of group soul mind which are less than pleasant to contemplate, such as the virus or plankton, and algae, but all play their part in the grand scheme of mind growth.

It may seem inconceivable as to how we progress from one level of mind to another, for at our present level of awareness it is difficult to imagine life as a worm, for instance. Yet there is more to mind expansion than we might imagine. In the earliest stages of mind growth the group may have had to learn to understand simply being in form. Then perhaps to experience physical development or growth, as all of nature does, to develop sensitivity, to move, to eat, to do all that has to be done in order to physically sustain the form. This could be as the insect that would feed on the plant, or vice versa, through to the animal that has to kill to feed itself, offspring or pack (or group).

Progression along the way teaches feelings, perhaps starting with immediate family or the same species. Then there is reason, the ability to think! Not simply to react or function according to one's nature, like a plant or tree that absorbs the moisture and nutrients from the ground (and even with this example, perhaps 'instinctive mind' is at work), but to actually think and decide on a course of action. The animal that hunts in the pack does this through joint cooperation, which is often little more than an instinctive, inherited memory of how to do so. Yet how did the instinct or inherited memory develop? By progression of the species some might say, but behind this is the mind, the developing mind of the species or group. It may well be that the same group developed greater understanding through a succession of incarnations in the same species form. So the descendants who benefited were the ancestors reborn! They had earned the right to progress through the improved form.

When mind reaches the highest point at which it can express in one form, it simply moves to the next appropriate life-stream. Not by choice, "I want to be this or that," but because it has progressed sufficiently to express at that next level of mind, (in a form where its level of awareness can further expand). So the next form it can express through will be one in which mind growth, or a greater understanding of self, becomes possible.

You may be wondering why your spirit essence was ever part of a group soul? There is a good reason, and the answer is because this enables equal progression for the entire group. As we all know, nature can seem very cruel; if at the group stage of development you had to rely upon self alone you may well have been left behind! You might, for instance, have been a daisy that was eaten by the cow every time you first reached the sunshine! While other daisies were learning what it was like to be blown by the breeze or gale force wind (perhaps early sensitivity, feeling and 'movement' learning) you could have been 'gone' and missed it all.

As part of a group, you share, because the group is one mind that has not yet reached the level of consciousness suitable for individualisation.

Mind is not limited by time and space. A collective or group mind can take multiple forms and be on different planes (some in physical form and some not) simultaneously.

Therefore if you or the aspect that eventually became you, missed out, you did not fall behind; all of the group learn what it is like to have the shortest stay as the daisy through to the longest. Such as the one which simply reaches the end of the form's natural lifespan. Thus the group moves forward together, from the bottom of the ladder to the pinnacle of the animal level.

At the top end of the animal scale are the forms that have human contact, such as the pet or companion animals. (I know that humans are really just higher animals or mammals, but for the sake of simplicity I am using "animal" to mean those below the human level of mind). At this stage the animals have not only developed emotional feelings and a reasonable degree of mental agility, as they progress towards greater self-awareness; many demonstrate a great love for their guardians. This is further drawn out of an animal by human caring and love.

It is when this is sufficiently developed that the indwelling soul reaches the next threshold, and can then progress to express through human form.

How long does all this take, you may well ask?

The answer is of course an x-factor. Nobody can say in absolute terms, for when you can appreciate eternity, why bother measuring durations? Also, time spans may vary greatly, for in eternity there is no rush!

What *can* be said, and this may help you to grasp eternity slightly better, is that your group origins could date back millions of years.

In one sense, of course, you have always existed, originally as an unconscious aspect of The Power. Although perhaps even "unconscious" may be an inadequate description? I'll leave you to ponder that one!

All I can say for sure, my friend, is that before you reached your present level of awareness, you, or your spirit essence, (as part of a group), had to expand your mind from the bottom rung of the vibrational ladder, through the experiences of myriads of incarnations, in an upward chain of progression.

Personally, it was in the late 1990's when I first conceived the idea of the evolution of the soul through lower life forms. Like many other people, in my earlier studies of spiritual knowledge, I had never given the subject any thought. However, at that point, I had perhaps reached a degree of understanding when I was ready to expand my knowledge. It is of course quite possible that my curiosity was aroused by the thoughts of my guides. Whatever the reason, my mind began to wonder about such things.

In my thoughts I began to question whether, for instance, a cat could ever be anything else but a cat. If it could never progress beyond that level of awareness, I concluded that their life would be rather limited. No matter how smart and loving the cat might become.

This did not sound fair to me; surely, I pondered, it cannot be all down to pot luck whether one is human, a cat, or some other life form.

At this stage I wanted clarification; my conscious mind was ready to receive the answer. So one quiet afternoon, while sitting alone in my former home in Alfred Street, Ryde, I attuned to my inner sensing in the hope of satisfying my curiosity.

Before long, everything became clear. I realised that if we can evolve and change physical form through reincarnation, and that alternative physical forms might be taken upon other planets, then clearly we can shift our consciousness through any number of physical forms.

Suddenly, the concept of spirit evolution through multiple different lower physical forms made complete sense to me; and the more I dwelt upon this 'revelation' the more obvious the fact seemed. After all, in basic terms, the human form is just another animal, albeit a more mentally advanced species. Other than the brain, we are only a step or two ahead of the primate, and share an almost identical DNA. So 'shifting' consciousness from one animal form to another is no big deal! We effectively do so whenever we reincarnate!

This understanding helped me to make greater sense of eternal life. The teaching that 'we are all born equal,' for instance, now made complete sense. When we realise that this relates to our outset, as droplets from the one ocean; we all start our consciousness growth at the bottom of the spirit ladder of evolution, at the slowest level of vibration. Nobody jumps the queue!

Since this time, my 'revelation' has been confirmed by a number of different spirit guides whose philosophy and teachings are encapsulated in a number of books, such as: *Nobody Wants to Listen – And Yet!,* by Sir Oliver Lodge (in spirit) spiritually transcribed by Raymond Smith. Many White Feather books, such as: *Truth From The White Brotherhood* - through the mediumship of Robert Goodwin, also confirm the evolution of the soul through all levels of form; as does the 1922 book: *The Consciousness of the Atom* by Alice Bailey. A spirit guide most appreciated by spiritualists, Silver Birch, also confirms this in such books as: *Lift Up Your Hearts*, where he says that "by love" we transfer to the animal the flame that enables the soul to progress to the human level of evolution.

One thing these teachings do is to confirm the interconnectedness of all life. It is another reason why we would be well advised to treat all life with reverence and respect. We have simply progressed further than some droplets from the ocean, and this does not make us better or more deserving; rather, it places more responsibility upon our shoulders.

## Individualised Soul Progression

The next stage of 'the journey of the soul' is the one at which you, and all human beings find ourselves; the level of individualised soul. You may have already been at the individualised level for thousands and thousands of years. If so, it is possible you have already experienced hundreds of human incarnations! The number of times you can return is limited only by whether potential new births match demand, and whether the likely births fit with your current soul plan (i.e. whether or not the circumstances would prove suitable for you to learn what you next seek and need to experience in order to advance your spirit evolution).

Naturally, most people would prefer to learn all that is necessary in as few physical lifetimes as possible. The knowledge that I am presenting to you could make a difference in this respect, because understanding of spiritual realities and natural laws encourages the possibility that people might live in the light of truth and express themselves accordingly. Then, perhaps, fewer incarnations would prove necessary?

Personally, I can't imagine how my life would have unfolded if I had not gathered the understanding that I now have. I find it most reassuring to know, without a shadow of doubt, that life is eternal and that we have so many friends and guides who seek to help us from the spirit world realms.

My chief guide is White Cloud, (I was going to say 'main' guide, but I thought I would 'promote' him to 'chief,' because it fits with his Native American lifetime!). To begin with he made contact through a number of different mediums, but originally the messages suggested that he was my twin brother! It drove me a little crazy (or crazier!) because his existence made no sense to my mother who was still upon earth at the time. It was another one of those tests of patience; he would explain when he was ready! Eventually, I was told his identity through an entranced medium, and this has since been confirmed on numerous occasions.

The reason why he communicated in this way was because we had been twins on numerous previous occasions during other physical lifetimes. During one, as young girls, we had been training in a temple, learning about sound vibrations. However, that lifetime was cut short when we passed in an earthquake. I was also his twin during the Indian lifetime, when I was apparently called: 'Silver Birch.' The latter name was also used by a teaching guide whose wisdom can be read in many books that you may enjoy reading, such as: *The Seed of Truth*, compiled by Tony Ortzen.

When I originally planned this lifetime as 'Jim,' White Cloud was again to be born as my twin. However, at the last minute, the plan was changed because he had cleared his karma and did not want to risk incurring more (who can blame him!). So White Cloud stayed in the spirit world and agreed to act as my guide. It was quite a while after I was told this that it dawned on me that I was obviously the weakest link! Although since then, I have been told that my own karma has now been cleared; but can I keep it that way, I wonder?

One other lifetime I would like to briefly share with you dates back to 1602, somewhere in Europe, when for a while I joined the Benedictine order of Monks. Peter, the Abbot I believe, informed me that the lifestyle did not suit me, so I did not remain with them for very long.

In spirit life, Peter and I are clearly still friends, and he has been confirmed on numerous occasions by many mediums, and was also sketched by spiritual artist Ivor James, a lovely man, who was most dedicated to the service that he provided.

Another spiritual artist, Raye Edwina Brown, produced a wonderful image of Red Cloud that, along with the image of Peter, you can see on my website gallery. It was also included on the back cover of an earlier edition of this book. I believe that Red Cloud might be a step ahead of White Cloud in the spirit realms. Although in his message which came with the artwork, it is clear that he also, has watched over me throughout this lifetime.

My friend, perhaps we can now expand the concept of eternity? Imagine spending the next hundred years in the spirit world realms; doing all that you fancy. Let us say, that you have always wanted to express yourself through art, painting landscapes and portraits, for instance. What an expert you would become after one hundred years, with tuition freely available from great masters of art. You would become a brilliant artist, I am sure.

Perhaps you might then enjoy helping a spiritual artist upon earth to draw portraits? All such mediums do have those who help them from the spirit world.

Eventually though, after a period of time, you would probably be looking for a new challenge. You would perhaps have had a glimpse of a higher level within the spirit world realms, and you would more than likely want to dwell there. You would have come to understand about your past lives and memories of them may have been awoken within you. You would also realise that it is only by once again reincarnating that greater awareness through experiences can help you to progress to that higher level. Therefore you seek to do so. This or a similar pattern may have been repeating itself time after time between incarnations.

Whether relatively quickly or after a long sojourn, there will undoubtedly come a time when you desire to experience the lessons that will help you to reach a higher frequency of vibration, and one that may enable you to dwell in that higher level of expression upon your next return to the spirit world realms. Although there is no guarantee, as the next earthly personality will have its own freewill consciousness.

This is just a snippet of what might be involved to move just a single step up the spiritual ladder. Measuring in earthly linear terms, 1000 years, 2000 years, 5000 years, even a hundred thousand years, is just a drop in the ocean of eternity. In comparison to your eternal journey such lengths of time are insignificant measurements. But then, time as we perceive it is irrelevant in eternity.

Earth is just one of countless planets upon which we can expand our mind through experiences. Although I understand that it is rare to switch planets midstream, as it were, unless a planet ceases to be suitable for your needs.

If the thought that you may previously, or at some point in the future could, incarnate upon another planet, seems rather mind-blowing, this is understandable. Yet, if you have grasped the concept of "eternity," and know without a shadow of doubt that thousands upon thousands of years from now, you will still exist and will still be progressing and seeking to move still further onwards upon the journey of the soul, then you may well have begun to realise that nothing, especially not in this timescale, is beyond possibility. We are aspects of The Power and our 'playground' of experience is not limited to the earthplane, and not for one brief visit, it is the universe and beyond, for *eternity*.

We are informed that there is countless life beyond the spirit world realms. The universe is the 'arena' of the soul, and in many ways, once we have progressed beyond the need for earthly incarnations and through the mind and spiritual realms to reach the 'dizzy' heights of the celestial realm (and this will be in the vast distances of time as we measure it) the adventures of eternity will have only just begun!

# Chapter Six
# Applying Spiritual Knowledge

My friend, you may wonder how spiritual knowledge can be applied to your present lifetime? Indeed, in many respects this is the most important aspect of all spiritual philosophy. Other than proving their survival it is the reason why those who communicate do so. To give us the knowledge of the wisdom they have gathered so that we might better conduct our lives, and thus progress more successfully than we might have done.

My advice is to bring your conscious thoughts back to the knowledge contained within these pages as regularly as you possibly can; especially during life's more stressful and difficult times, as that is when it will benefit you the most. Hopefully, it will encourage you to be even more forgiving, tolerant, and compassionate, and also more readily able to cope with bereavement.

Our Native American friends have an expression which you may have heard before? Something along the lines of: 'You've talked the talk, now it is time to walk the walk.' In this case, we can say that intellectual knowledge is meaningless unless we can apply the truth to our lives. We need to not only speak the truth, but be the truth, by the way that we live our lives; by the way that we treat others, and ourselves; by endeavouring to be the caring, sharing, and loving souls which at the core of our inner being we are.

# Suffering

My friend, when we see or personally experience suffering, it is natural for us to hope and pray that it will soon end. Yet pain and suffering, difficulty and hardship, all play an important part in the evolution of the human soul. Many people, even during their current lifetime, can look back and see that often their greatest crises or most difficult problems, their darkest hours, helped to make them more compassionate and understanding towards others.

You could not evolve if you lived totally free from care, anxiety and worry; where every difficulty was removed so that it never touched you and where there was nothing for you to overcome, face or rise above. It is through adversity, suffering in so many ways, that we grow. All suffering brings its own reward because it touches the soul and, in so doing, gives it greater awareness of the higher and deeper aspects of life and a more profound understanding of self.

Every experience is part of the tapestry of your life; if you try to judge whether it is fair or not, you will be judging with limited physical vision. It is a fact that a thread runs throughout all lifetimes, bringing the experiences which will quicken your soul vibration.

The darkness and the light, the shadow and the sunshine, are all reflections of the whole. Without light there could be no shadow, but without shadow we could not appreciate the light. The difficulties of life are steps which enable the soul to climb higher. The events in your life may at times seem harsh, bringing you despair, pain and misery, but all play their part in teaching and enhancing soul growth.

Many people, intent in wallowing in self-pity, say, 'you don't know what it is like, unless you've been through it yourself.' They do not realise that they have touched upon a great and most important truth. At a deeper level of soul consciousness we *cannot* truly appreciate the emotions without personal physical experience, and this is precisely *why* we choose to incarnate and endeavour to learn from the harsher realities of earthly life. Whether we manage to learn and grow from our experiences depends largely upon how we react, which naturally is our own freewill choice. Do we choose to remain attached to self-pity, or do we move forward with courage and become a better person and an example that others may wish to emulate?

Difficulties, obstacles and handicaps, are all trials of the soul. When they are overcome the soul rises to become more highly evolved. Your experiences are all part of your evolution. One day, in spirit, you will look back in retrospect and view the lifetimes you have lived on earth. From the jigsaw of all the events, of multiple lifetimes, you will see how every piece fits together, and how every experience was a lesson to quicken the soul and to enable it to have greater understanding of its possibilities.

We are told that there is no experience which comes to the human soul that, when rightly understood and rightly faced, does not leave you better for it. I truly hope that in understanding this it will at least give you some solace and reason to appreciate the lessons which your life experiences present to you. If you can recognise the challenges, be grateful for them, as they are the stepping stones which you have chosen to experience as part of your life plan, and by which you may reach a higher level of expression.

## Forgiveness

My friend, our spirit friends encourage us to develop a forgiving nature for a number of reasons. By so doing we release the negative energies which can be generated when we hold emotional states such as anger, hatred and resentment within. When we hold such feelings within our emotional and mental energy fields (or aura), this can cause disharmony at a physical level of being, as the physical is so often an expression of how we think.

I can understand that it is far from easy for those who have been subjected to any major trauma in life, such as cruelty and abuse, or for someone who loses a loved one by an act of murder or drunken driving, for example, to be forgiving. At such times it may help to remind one's self that nobody truly 'dies.' Nobody ever has or ever will!

Spiritual knowledge teaches us that every seeming 'victim' is released to transcend to a higher and far superior state of being; to a level that befits their personal level of progression. *All* suffering: physical, emotional or mental, is transient; a blip in time to the eternal soul, but as painful as it may be to us (at the physical level of consciousness), it may be helping to teach a valued lesson to one, or more, souls.

My friend, remember also that no one knows what *they* may have done in past lifetimes. We also do not know the pathway which has helped to shape the character of another. Whether it has been one which we might consider 'normal' or one that has seen them enduring who knows what. You would not wish to be judged for what you did in a previous incarnation. The past cannot be changed, but your future can. No one 'escapes' the consequences of universal law. However, for our own sake, we would be well advised not to judge, and whenever possible, to forgive.

## Bereavement

My friend, you may have encountered bereavement in your lifetime; when a loved one or dear friend returns to reside in the spirit world realms. Grief is natural, to an extent, for we do miss their physical presence. But if you successfully apply spiritual knowledge to your present lifetime, you will be able to cope more readily. The greatest sadness of all is ignorance. It would be so much better if people could replace hope and faith with knowledge.

Whether the loss is expected or not, my advice to you is to keep reminding yourself that you, and they, are an eternal soul. They have simply gone ahead of you to a realm which is more glorious than any reality that we experience upon this earthplane.

I am aware that it is far from easy to keep spiritual realities uppermost in one's thoughts and not to be swept along by the everyday physical events of life.

One has to constantly bring one's thoughts back to the reason for incarnation, and to effectively retune to the greater truth. Naturally, it would be far better if this knowledge were known before the occasion of any bereavement.

A physical transition often heralds a time of celebration in the spirit life. The occasion is the return to the true home, from a sojourn upon the earthplane. It signifies that you may very well have achieved all that you came for and that your purpose in this lifetime has been fulfilled. Although it is true to say that some lifetimes *are* cut shorter than the pre-birth life plan by 'unscheduled' physical intervention. This, quite obviously, can happen because we all have freewill. However, it is not the end of life; it is the beginning of a new chapter.

Eternal life is a constant and continuous adventure that has many beginnings, but no true end. 'Wisdom is not recognising truth, it is *living* by it.' I thoroughly recommend that you try very hard to take this statement to heart, to make it part of your own philosophy of life, for it will serve you well.


# Courage

My friend, for many and perhaps all people, life incarnate is a test of courage. This is particularly so for those people who live in areas of the world where poverty and starvation are widespread. The courage that life demands from them principally relates to their physical survival, to shelter, food and water; although their emotions and mental strength must also be tested to the core. Perhaps their courage helps to teach those of us with less traumatic lives to be more grateful for our own lot?

Everything in life is, of course, relevant to your circumstances, and what you become used to. Therefore, in the West, where the vast majority of people live reasonably comfortable lives, the courage that we may need to find within ourselves, (although this can be of a physical nature) more often *is* of the emotional and mental kind. Can we face tomorrow when we lose a loved one, or when a husband, wife or partner walks out on us? Have we the faith to believe that at some time in our future we may find another with whom to share happiness? Even, perhaps in some originally unforeseen way, that we will find satisfaction in something else?

When we lose a job and may be our home as a result, can we retain hope that something more fulfilling might materialise and trust that there is a purpose to all things? Can we find joy in the simple things of life, such as a walk in the fresh air and hearing the sounds of nature with the songs that the birds sing, realising that happiness is a state of mind? Can we let go of unnecessary possessions which may in fact be a burden to us?

Can we, at all times, be honest with ourselves and others? Can we avoid temptation and remain pure in heart, and follow our conscience at all times? Have we the integrity to live according to our convictions? Do we 'live and let live' without interfering in the lives of others? Do we live as responsible human beings? Are we dedicated to truth, whatever our understanding of this is?

Everything in life takes courage, of one sort or another. By recognising that all experiences are necessary for soul growth, it will help you to gather knowledge and strength of character, and this will benefit your spiritual progression. We also need to love and respect ourselves; to remember that we too are worthy, and that we have a right to be here. Can we also be the courageous soul, the one who leads by example?

## Gratitude

My friend, I would ask you to attune to an inner state of gratitude for the life which you lead. To be grateful that in this lifetime you do not live in a country where life is a constant struggle for survival; where children have to beg, borrow, steal or perish on the streets, experiencing little if any love, comfort or lasting pleasure.

I know that there are people in this country who experience traumatic, sad and abusive childhoods, and for various reasons a number of them become homeless, but physical life for the majority of us, is comparatively comfortable.

Many people take it for granted that they can afford to purchase adequate provisions to feed themselves, and that with the flick of a switch they can have light and power for appliances. If you can focus on being grateful for this, and grateful for the simple things in life; for your friendships and the love that you share; for the flowers and the trees; for the birds and their songs; for the unconditional love freely offered to you by cats, dogs, and other friends from the animal kingdom; and for the gift of life itself. We have in this lifetime been given the opportunity to grow, to increase our deeper spiritual understanding so that we might raise or quicken our personal energy vibrations, and for this we can also be grateful.

I know that what I have said here is not 'news' to you, because modern media coverage informs people of the plight of others. Yet I feel it is worth mentioning, so that you may use it to remind yourself of the need to be grateful that this is not your situation in this lifetime. Although people who have clinical depression and other illnesses or disabilities may find it difficult to feel grateful, it will hopefully not prove impossible for them to do so; especially if they can remind themselves that they may well have agreed to their life challenges in order to enhance their soul growth.

Generally speaking, I would suggest that whenever you feel sad in life, attune yourself to an inner state of gratitude by reminding yourself of the good things in your life.

## Peace and Unconditional Love

My friend, if we can cultivate qualities of a peaceful nature within ourselves, so that the petty things of this world do not disturb our equilibrium, this will greatly enhance our spiritual progression.

If we can also express unconditional love, as we recognise that all people, of all nations and races, are our brothers and sisters, other kindred souls, who also seek progression upon the spiritual pathway, then we will be doubly blessed. As you might expect, I feel that this recognition also needs to be extended to the animal kingdom and to the world of nature.

You may wonder how you can find a meaningful state of inner peace, in a world that lacks equality and remains so cruel, and I recognise that it is not an easy thing to do. But how can the world find peace and become a planet where love abounds if individuals cannot find it within themselves? The vibrations, the planetary energies, follow the people. They are fashioned by how we think and live.

If you can find a state of inner peace, either through meditation, or maybe by walking in the countryside or a park (where there are trees), it will bring healing to the soul, and will help you to overcome the harshness of life.

The age that we have entered, the Aquarian age, is said to be one of enlightenment, a golden age. However, this can only be ushered in by the raising of individual energy vibrations. As you may have gathered from reading about the evolution of the soul, nothing in creation happens overnight.

Those of us presently upon earth are the pioneers of a new age. We can take things as far as personal and collective limits allow, then we must pass the responsibility on to those who follow us.

Please do try to remember at all times the spiritual truths, that life is eternal, that nobody truly dies, and that life is a learning experience which we ourselves have volunteered to undertake; it is one way that you can help yourself find a state of inner peace. You may not retain it for every second of every day, but you can begin the process, and hopefully retune yourself to a balanced state on a regular basis. In this way your example will inspire, and thus enable, future generations to advance the process still further. Then the world will find greater and greater peace.

Our spirit teachers tell us that creation, the universe itself, is an expression of love; that all energy is an aspect of love. Yet the essence of love within each of us is so often buried beneath the fabric (the material overcoat), in which we place ourselves.

We take on a personality, an ego, when we incarnate, and this is often far removed from the real us, the soul essence. This may seem unfortunate, but as you have read, it is a necessary process if we are to progress to higher levels of expression. Yet, if we can dig deep within ourselves and connect with our inner being, which links with our higher self, we will discover a nobler, finer side to ourselves. This is what we need to connect with, through conscience and intuition, and then we may express facets of unconditional love in our daily lives.

You can then extend to all others the same love that you hold for those dear to you, as you recognise that everyone else in this world is an equally deserving soul. Their spiritual identity may be buried beneath the ego, yet within each of us the spark of the divine still burns. At present, it may appear brighter in some than in others; and yet even in those where the glow of their inner light seems but a mere flicker, it can never be extinguished, and is waiting to be rekindled by the fuel of love.

Every soul is your equal; in a sense, they are you and you are they, for we are all droplets from the one ocean of eternal life. When sufficient numbers of people can appreciate this, then greater equality will be extended to all nations and races of this world. Then we will all be able to live in peace, and be free to express our inner creativity, gifts, abilities and love.

## Service

My friend, as you gather spiritual knowledge to apply to your own life, you can also serve and help others by spreading the truth and wisdom of these teachings.

Speaking generally, I believe that people are becoming more aware and receptive to this knowledge, although throughout the world many still live in darkness and despair. They cannot see the purpose of their existence and live in a constant state of uncertainty and worry. Perhaps you can help them to understand their true nature and enlighten them to the spiritual facts of life and universal laws?

Even if you can only plant a seed of truth into their minds, you will be doing them a great service. At first their response might be indifference, perhaps even scornful, but some time later, their mind may start to open and they might become more receptive to the truth. Then they may seek you out in order to gain greater understanding. Always remember that words of wisdom, like loving thoughts and prayers, are never wasted.

So many people ignore genuine spiritual education; perhaps they confuse it with the dogmatic teachings of the various religions which base their beliefs upon faith? As a result they go through their life blinkered, not seeing its value, and how it can give meaning to their life.

You will be performing a wonderful service if you can bring knowledge where there is ignorance, joy where there is sorrow, hope where there is despair, love where there is hatred, and peace where there is conflict.

Let the wisdom you gather be your guiding light, and let the truth sustain you on your journey through life. Radiate your light with kindness, generosity of spirit, love and compassion and you will help to brighten this world of ours, and set a good example for others to follow.

## Motive and Ego

My friend, I would like to remind you that the motives behind your actions have an effect upon your karmic balance. It is a responsible person who questions themselves about the motive behind every action which they plan; and a wise person who proceeds only if their conscience tells them that it is pure of heart. If you can live by this code of conduct, your karmic balance is unlikely to be disturbed. Those, whose motives are selfish or greedy, seeking power and control, or to elevate themselves in some way, will reap accordingly.

As the intellect grows, one aspect of earthly

consciousness which needs careful self-monitoring is the ego. Many individuals and organisations convince themselves that they 'know best,' and wish to establish or maintain a position of 'power' and 'control.' One example is the overbearing mother or father who tries to manipulate or even dominate how their children live, rather than encourage and guide them, and this can sometimes be carried through into adulthood.

There are a great number of people in the world who have inflated egos or the 'big brother' mentality, from parents, teachers and clergy, to doctors, bureaucrats and governments. Once given or permitted the authority to 'direct' or 'govern,' many become convinced of their own infallibility. Therefore, in addition to monitoring yourself, so that you avoid creating any karmic imbalance, it may also be advisable to guard against being the one who is manipulated or dominated by others. If you use your intuition to question everything that does not 'feel' right, you will often see through what you are being told so that you can discover whether an inflated ego or a hidden agenda is lurking.

## Money

My friend, I would suggest that money *is not* the driving force and most important consideration behind how you live your life. Many people spend their lives in pursuit of money ('success,' wealth) and equate this with happiness. Yet happiness is an inner state of mind. When you are aware of the spiritual facts of life, you can be perfectly happy with the simple things in life. Life in the physical world requires sufficient food and water, adequate clothing and shelter, and funds to cover the costs of these, plus a little more so that we can express ourselves and pursue hobbies and so forth. However, we do not need vast reserves and great mansions to live in.

Often it is fear or greed which drives so many people along the materialistic pathways. The fear that they must 'save for a rainy day' is understandable to a degree, but so often this is taken to extremes which become detrimental to the expression of the indwelling soul, because they stop living life in the way that their soul intends. Why be fearful, when you know that you are an immortal being?

Those who are greedy, so often have a blinkered outlook on life which only allows them to see in the direction of physical gratification, and this, inevitably, is contrary to the desires of their soul.

Many people become confused about money and spiritual realities. There is even a teaching that purports to be spiritual which in most cases succeeds only in encouraging the pursuit of material desires. It suggests that we need only to be sufficiently 'positive' and project to the 'universe' (meaning the Power, God, the Great Spirit) the image of money, wealth, or whatever else we desire coming to us, for this to empower it to manifest. This teaching lacks the broader understanding of how the spiritual universe operates, and therefore is very misleading and will only succeed in disappointing most people.

Developing a positive frame of mind is certainly desirable, and thoughts do create. This is certainly so on a higher frequency of vibration in spirit life. Upon earth, it can also take effect; for example, if you send out the thought (the mind wave) that you *need* (rather than 'want') something, this will connect at a higher level of consciousness with other souls upon earth who are at a similar level of thought vibration. Consciously they are unlikely to realise this, but at a higher level of being they may be able to respond and prompt their physical self to be of service. Scientifically, this can be described as a sub-atomic link. The result can be to draw to yourself those people who will help you, or for the object that you seek to 'manifest.' Perhaps someone will offer it to you, or you will unexpectedly stumble across it in a charity shop, for instance.

However, nothing is guaranteed, it may be that what you seek is outside the orbit of your physical life. The broader truth of how the spiritual universe operates also teaches us to consider the outworking of karma and your soul's plan for this incarnation. Life would be very easy if all we had to do was to learn the art of sufficient positive thought for all of our desires to magically manifest. If this was the case, and all our dreams could so readily become reality, what would we learn and accomplish? Life, of course, does not 'work' in this way. It never has and it never will. Our karma and life plan cannot be overridden by thought, and at a soul level of consciousness, we recognise this.

There is nothing 'wrong' with money in itself; it is a convenient bartering tool. Yet, at the end of the day (physical passing), it is not money that we take with us on our return journey to the spirit dimensions, it is experience – what we have learned at a soul level. One ounce of wisdom is therefore worth far more than a sack full of gold.

One final thought for you to consider is that some people, in their life plan, do choose to experience having an abundance of money. They may have had many previous lifetimes where they have struggled to survive and have therefore earned the right to experience an easier life in this respect (but not necessarily in all respects). While another person could plan wealth as a 'test' to see how wisely they might handle the responsibility that it can bestow. Will their wealth be used with compassion, kindness and consideration for others, or purely for their own pleasure? At a soul level of consciousness, I can guess which choice they hope and plan to make upon earth, but will their earthly personality follow the promptings of their soul?

## Humour

My friend, there is one more matter which I feel is important to mention. Life, as we all know, can at times be hard to bear. The world can be a cruel and seemingly unforgiving place; yet it still retains great beauty and offers so much to enjoy. Whenever you get the opportunity, please, my friend, *do* enjoy it. Grab each moment of love, happiness and pleasure that you can.

The life plan of many souls is to lighten this world through humour. Comedians are often fulfilling the desires of their soul and providing a great service for this world. Song writers and musicians, artists and poets, and many others in all fields of creative expression are likewise inspiring and uplifting others. Please *do* absorb the love, beauty and humour that they provide; and this will help to lighten your pathway through life. Try to find something to laugh about everyday; or better still, every hour!

Life is serious to a point, we do have our responsibilities, and we need to experience whatever we came here to learn. At the same time, there are always moments in life which can be enjoyed. Why should we take things *too* seriously, when we know that life is eternal?

My friend, please do try to find the humour of the soul that truly does lie within you, to laugh at life, and this may help to cushion those harsher moments. I mentioned earlier that a sense of humour is certainly retained by those who communicate with us. Some of the guides and helpers have a dry wit, while others are more unmistakably humorous.

In addition to the guides who teach and share their philosophy and wisdom, I have spoken to others who come specifically to lighten the atmosphere with their humour. They do so because this raises the energies, which in turn can make communication a little easier for them.

Mary, a spirit guide who acts as 'doorkeeper' (a soul who oversees who can communicate) to one trance medium I know, said that in her past incarnation, around the time of the Battle of

Trafalgar (21$^{st}$ October, 1805), she 'entertained gents, or the girls did!' She was the 'madam' of a brothel in Portsmouth! No doubt trade was brisk, with many sailors coming and going during times of conflict, such as the Napoleonic Wars (1799-1815). Nelson himself sailed from Portsmouth onboard HMS Victory to command the battle.

A typical remark from Mary is that she 'will have no riffraff (disreputable persons) coming through,' and, 'no swearing,' because she now regards herself as a more dignified lady!

A couple of spirit gentlemen are also very amusing, and opposites in many ways. One is definitely a 'ladies man,' and he openly admits to preferring those ladies who are 'well built' (I am using more polite terms). He has also told us that he is on the lookout for another wife, as the one that he has in the spirit world, in earthly terms, is now getting old!

The other spirit gentleman is perhaps the most outrageous and hilarious spirit helper to communicate; he jokingly tries to ignore any lady present! On one occasion, he told us that he did have a gentleman friend (in his past incarnation) but the 'poor chap' had to marry 'some female' (possibly an 'arranged' marriage), adding, 'How ghastly for him!'

This is just a snippet of some of the humorous moments. My point being, that life needs to be enjoyed whenever possible. Those who are progressed in the spirit world recognise this need; they do not become pious or 'holier-than-thou' in attitude.

# Farewell

My friend, within these pages I have touched upon a number of teachings that can be termed 'Spiritual Knowledge.' Some you might wish to seek further clarification upon, while you may also have other questions that remain unanswered?

Let me assure you that answers to every conceivable question can very often be found quite easily by any earnest seeker. So if you do want or need to know more, I would encourage you to seek with an open but discerning mind, allowing your intuition to guide you towards genuine spiritual knowledge, truth and wisdom.

Enjoy the experiences that are ahead of you.

In truth, love and light…

From your friend,

*James McQuitty*

# About the Author

James McQuitty was born in Putney, London. He moved to Ryde, Isle of Wight in 1992 and has lived there ever since. He has studied spiritual philosophy since 1981, and became an author upon the release of his first book: *Golden Enlightenment* in 1994.

James' writing 'mission' was inspired by a message received through trance communication. He is also a spiritual healer.

James currently undertakes speaking engagements to share his understanding with a wider audience.

**www.jamesmcquitty.com**

8321008R00054

Printed in Great Britain
by Amazon.co.uk, Ltd.,
Marston Gate.